Columbus Day

Molly
Aloian

Crabtree Publishing Company

www.crabtreebooks.com

Crabtree Publishing Company
www.crabtreebooks.com

Author: Molly Aloian
Coordinating editor: Chester Fisher
Series editor: Susan LaBella
Editor: Adrianna Morganelli
Proofreader: Reagan Miller
Editorial director: Kathy Middleton
Production coordinator: Katherine Berti
Prepress technician: Katherine Berti
Project manager: Kumar Kunal (Q2AMEDIA)
Art direction: Rahul Dhiman (Q2AMEDIA)
Cover design: Cheena Yadav (Q2AMEDIA)
Design: Cheena Yadav (Q2AMEDIA)
Photo research: Debabrata Sen (Q2AMEDIA)

Photographs:
AP Photo: Richard Drew: p. 20; Arnulfo Franco: p. 26; Marty
    Lederhandler: cover (main image), p. 14; Edward Troon: p. 27
Big Stock Photo: Ciprian Dumitrescu: p. 22
Corbis: Morton Beebe: p. 21; K. J. Historical: p. 19 (painting)
Dreamstime: Enrico Battilana: p. 31; Parrypix: p. 4; Etoile Pinder:
    p. 8; Toddtaulman: p. 15
Flickr: PhareannaH: p. 24
Fotolia: Peppejoe: p. 23
Getty Images: Spencer Platt/Staff: p. 18; Spanish School: p. 7
Istockphoto: Artemis Gordon: p. 29
Library of Congress: p. 6, 17
Photolibrary: The Bridgeman Art Library: p. 10; North Wind Pictures:
    p. 12, 13; The Print Collector: p. 11; Visions LLC: p. 5
Reuters: STR New: p. 9
Shutterstock: cover (background); p. 1; Stasys Eidiejus: p. 30 (map);
    Gelpi: p. 19 (children); Iofoto: p. 30 (girl); Emin Kuliyev: p. 16;
    Taipan Kid: folio image

Library and Archives Canada Cataloguing in Publication

Aloian, Molly
        Columbus Day / Molly Aloian.

(Celebrations in my world)
Includes index.
ISBN 978-0-7787-4760-4 (bound).--ISBN 978-0-7787-4778-9 (pbk.)

        1. Columbus, Christopher--Juvenile literature. 2. Columbus Day--
Juvenile literature. 3. America--Discovery and exploration--Spanish--
Juvenile literature. I. Title. II. Series: Celebrations in my world

E120.A46 2009   j394.264   C2009-905257-1

Library of Congress Cataloging-in-Publication Data

Aloian, Molly.
 Columbus Day / Molly Aloian.
      p. cm. -- (Celebrations in my world)
 Includes index.
 ISBN 978-0-7787-4778-9 (pbk. : alk. paper) -- ISBN 978-0-7787-4760-4
(reinforced library binding : alk. paper)
1. Columbus Day--Juvenile literature. 2. Columbus, Christopher--Juvenile
literature. 3. America--Discovery and exploration--Spanish--Juvenile
literature. I. Title. II. Series.

 E120.A45 2010
 394.264--dc22

                                        2009034878

Crabtree Publishing Company

www.crabtreebooks.com   1-800-387-7650

Printed in China/122009/CT20090915

Published in Canada
Crabtree Publishing
616 Welland Ave.
St. Catharines, ON
L2M 5V6

Published in the United States
Crabtree Publishing
350 Fifth Ave.
59th floor
New York, NY 10118

Published in the United Kingdom
Crabtree Publishing
Maritime House
Basin Road North, Hove
BN41 1WR

Published in Australia
Crabtree Publishing
386 Mt. Alexander Rd.
Ascot Vale (Melbourne)
VIC 3032

Contents

What is Columbus Day?

Columbus Day is a holiday. People celebrate Columbus Day on October 12 of each year. This day is the anniversary of the day that a famous explorer named Christopher Columbus arrived on lands in what is now America.

- Flying the American flag is a great way to celebrate Columbus Day.

These people are at a Columbus Day celebration.

DID YOU KNOW?

Christopher Columbus lived more than 500 years ago. On Columbus Day, people celebrate the history of the United States. It is a day to feel patriotic, or proud of your country.

Who Was Christopher Columbus?

Christopher Columbus was born in Genoa, which is a city in Italy. His father was a wool **merchant**. His mother was the daughter of a wool weaver.

● This is a portrait of Christopher Columbus.

DID YOU KNOW?

As a child, Christopher Columbus had little education and could not read or write.

6

As a young man, Columbus dreamed of becoming a sailor.

Columbus wanted to sail west to cross the Atlantic Ocean to Asia. He wanted to trade goods for spices, gold, and silk. But Columbus needed money for his journey. He asked King Ferdinand and Queen Isabella of Spain for money for the trip.

- King Ferdinand and Queen Isabella promised Columbus that he could rule any lands he found on his journey.

Queen Isabella

7

Four Voyages

Columbus hired a crew of sailors from Spain. Columbus and his crew made four **voyages** across the Atlantic Ocean. They began their first voyage in 1492. When they spotted land, they believed that they had reached Asia. They were actually on a small island in the Bahamas. Columbus named the island San Salvador.

● A cross on San Salvador Island marks the spot where many think Columbus first landed.

Columbus visited many new lands on his voyages. He visited the present-day countries of Cuba, Haiti, and the Dominican Republic. He also explored the coastlines of many other countries. On his third voyage, he explored South America.

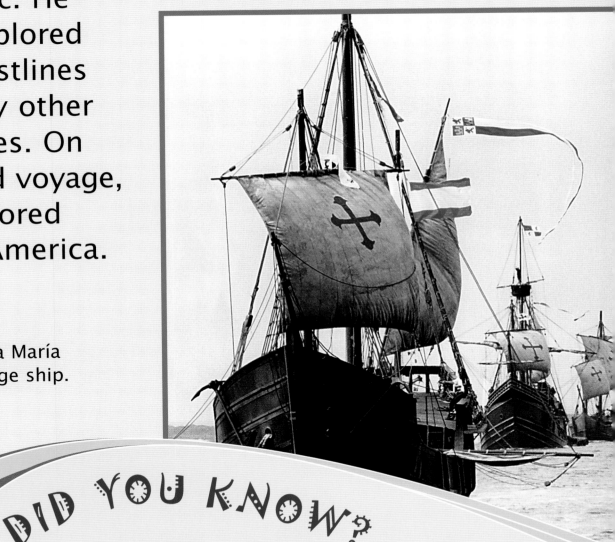

- The Santa María was a large ship.

DID YOU KNOW?

Columbus and his crew sailed three ships. They were the Niña, *the* Pinta, *and the* Santa María. *The* Santa María *was the largest and slowest. It was Columbus'* **flagship**.

9

Discovering the New World

People in Europe called these new lands the New World. Today, Christopher Columbus is known for discovering the New World. People celebrate his discoveries because he opened up the Americas to European **settlement**.

At first, Columbus believed America was Asia.

There were Native peoples, including the Taino and the Carib, living on the lands of the New World. They lived in villages. The Taino and the Carib were bitter enemies.

The Taino greeted Columbus and his crew when they first arrived.

DID YOU KNOW?

Columbus is known for discovering the Americas, but a Viking named Leif Eriksson visited North America for the first time 500 years earlier.

11

Many Changes

Columbus' arrival in the New World changed life for the Native peoples. Columbus and the Spanish believed that the Native people were **uncivilized**. They **mistreated** the Native people and forced them into **slavery**.

The Spanish forced the Native peoples to be slaves.

Columbus and his crew were Christians. The Native peoples practiced other religions, however. Columbus and the Spanish explorers forced the Native peoples to **convert** to Christianity. They also forced them to leave their villages.

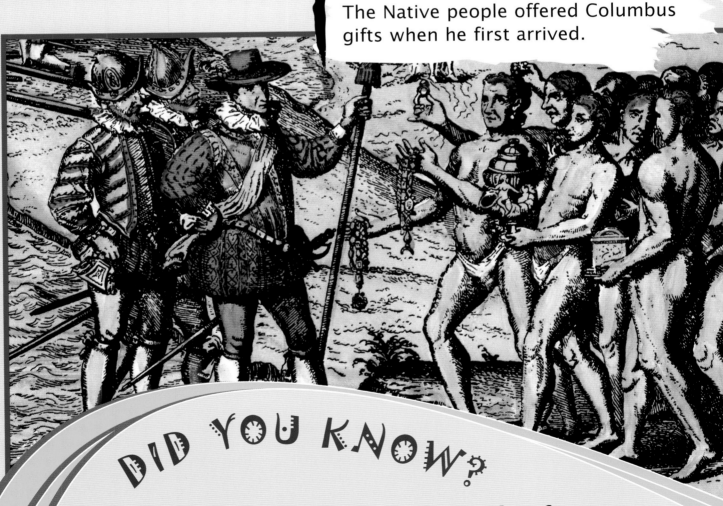

The Native people offered Columbus gifts when he first arrived.

DID YOU KNOW?

The Carib lived in houses with wooden frames covered with leaves, reeds, and straw. They packed mud to make floors in their houses.

13

Why Celebrate?

People celebrate Columbus Day because his arrival in the New World led to the **colonization** of North America and South America. People want to honor Columbus and his discoveries because they are important in the history of the United States.

On Columbus Day, people in the United States commemorate Christopher Columbus.

Columbus Day is celebrated in the United States.

In 1905, Colorado became the first state to celebrate Columbus Day. Columbus Day became a **federal** holiday in 1970.

- The city of Columbus in Ohio is named after Christopher Columbus.

DID YOU KNOW?

During the 1400s, people did not know much about the world. Many people believed that the Earth was flat.

15

Early Celebrations

In 1792, people in New York City and other eastern cities in the United States celebrated the 300th anniversary of Columbus' landing in the Americas. There was a special ceremony during the celebration.

One hundred years later in 1892, a statue of Columbus was raised at the beginning of Columbus Avenue in New York City.

● This statue of Christopher Columbus is in New York City.

DID YOU KNOW?

Christopher Columbus was sometimes called the "Admiral of the Ocean Sea." An admiral is a commander.

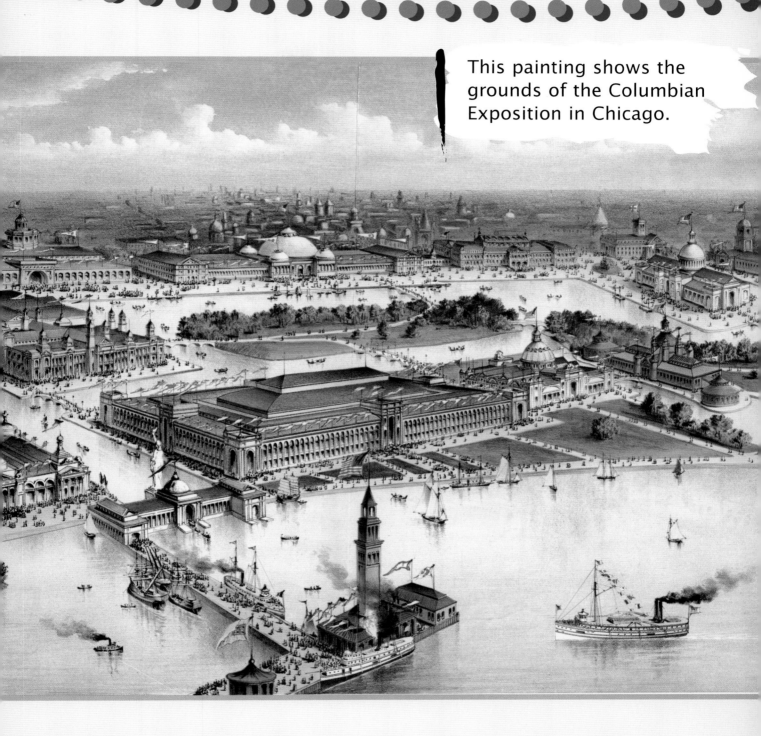

This painting shows the grounds of the Columbian Exposition in Chicago.

The next year, **replicas** of Columbus' three ships were displayed at the Columbian Exposition in Chicago.

Celebrate Today!

Today's Columbus Day celebrations include special decorations, parades, foods, and other activities. There are many ways to celebrate Columbus Day.

- These people wave the flag of Italy on Columbus Day.

DID YOU KNOW?

The country of Colombia in South America is named after Christopher Columbus.

These children are making Columbus Day posters.

Get creative when you are thinking of ways to celebrate Columbus Day at your home or school.

You can make a Columbus Day poster or mural to hang in your classroom. Get other students involved, too! The poster or mural will remind everyone of the importance of celebrating Columbus Day.

Parades

Many cities hold Columbus Day parades. Baltimore, Maryland, claims to have the "Oldest Continuous Marching Parade in America" celebrating Columbus Day. In 2008, Denver, Colorado, held its 101st Columbus Day parade.

● These people are at a Columbus Day parade in New York City.

DID YOU KNOW?

There is a United States one-cent postage stamp featuring Christopher Columbus.

● This man is
   dressed in
   costume for
   Columbus Day.

There are floats, marching bands,
and people dressed in costumes in
Columbus Day parades.

The floats often look like Columbus'
ships. Some people may be dressed
up like Columbus' crew members or
Columbus himself!

21

Foods

Many people eat Italian foods on Columbus Day because Christopher Columbus was born in Italy. Italian Americans want to honor Columbus and his **heritage**. People eat pizza, pasta, olives, cheese, and other Italian foods.

● Eating Italian food is one way to celebrate Columbus Day.

Columbus discovered new foods, including sweet potatoes, kidney beans, and maize, on the island known today as Cuba.

For this year's Columbus Day celebration, pretend you are part of Columbus' crew and eat a sailor's meal of salted meats, sardines, olives, peas, cheese, and raisins. Crew members often ate only one meal a day and they ate with their hands!

Olives were part of the crew's diet.

23

Songs and Rhymes

Some people sing songs on Columbus Day. Singing songs with friends or family is a fun way to celebrate this holiday.

These children are singing a Columbus Day song.

DID YOU KNOW?

Columbus called his fourth and final voyage "el alto viaje," which meant "the high voyage." He had high hopes that he would finally discover a route to Asia.

One Columbus Day song
begins like this:

In fourteen hundred ninety-two
Columbus sailed the ocean blue.
He had three ships and left from Spain;
He sailed through sunshine, wind, and rain.
He sailed by night; he sailed by day;
He used the stars to find his way.

- The word blue rhymes with the word two.

This rhyme will help you remember
the year of Columbus' first voyage:
Columbus sailed the ocean blue
in 1492.

25

Around the World

People all over the world celebrate Columbus Day. There are big celebrations in cities in Spain and Italy. Many countries in Latin America celebrate Columbus Day as Día de la Raza, which means "Day of the Race" or "Day of the People."

12 DE OCTUBRE DÍA DE LA HISPANIDAD

These people are celebrating Columbus Day in Barcelona, Spain.

DID YOU KNOW?

In Costa Rica, people celebrate Día de las Culturas or "Day of the Cultures" on Columbus Day.

This picture shows an Indigenous Peoples Day celebration.

Some people who celebrate Día de la Raza honor the **indigenous** peoples of Latin America. They celebrate the culture that developed over the centuries as their heritage mixed with that of the Spanish explorers who followed Columbus.

Columbus Day Activities

There are many Columbus Day activities that can make your celebration even more fun. Print out a map of the Caribbean and draw the courses of Columbus' four voyages to the New World. Make a Columbus Day crossword puzzle to give to your friends and family.

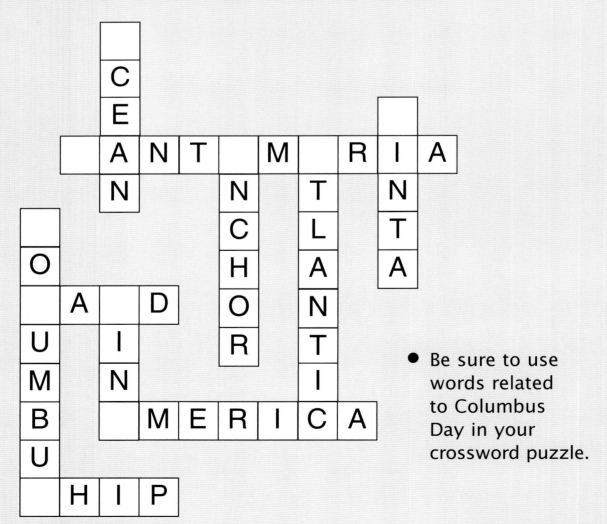

- Be sure to use words related to Columbus Day in your crossword puzzle.

- You could read your poem to your friends when you are finished.

Write down five words related to Columbus Day and then write a sentence using each word. You and your friends can write a poem about Christopher Columbus. Each line should start with a letter from the word "Columbus."

DID YOU KNOW?

Christopher Columbus is called Cristobal Colon in Spanish. He is called Cristovio Colombo in Portuguese. In Italian, he is called Cristoforo Colombo.

Learn More!

Learn more about Christopher Columbus and why it is important to celebrate Columbus Day each year. Visit the library and read books about Columbus and his voyages. Share what you learn with your family and friends.

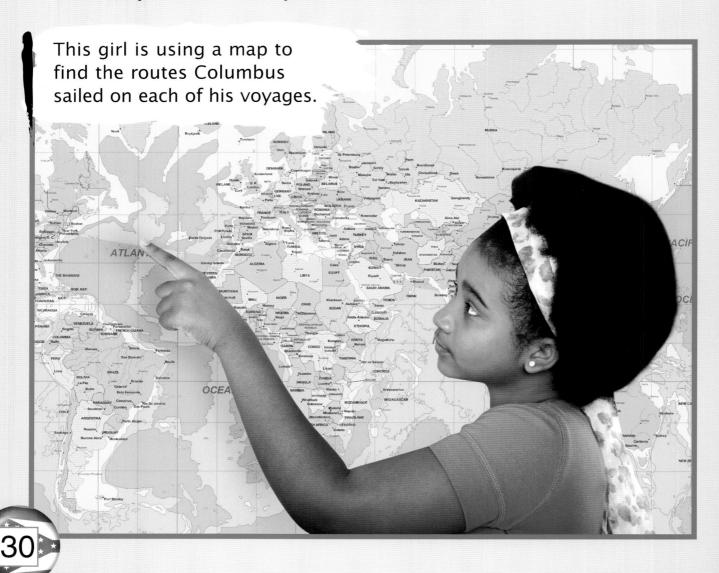

This girl is using a map to find the routes Columbus sailed on each of his voyages.

Make a Columbus Day quiz or word search to give to your family and friends. Here is a question to help you start your quiz: When was the first recorded celebration of Columbus Day in the United States?

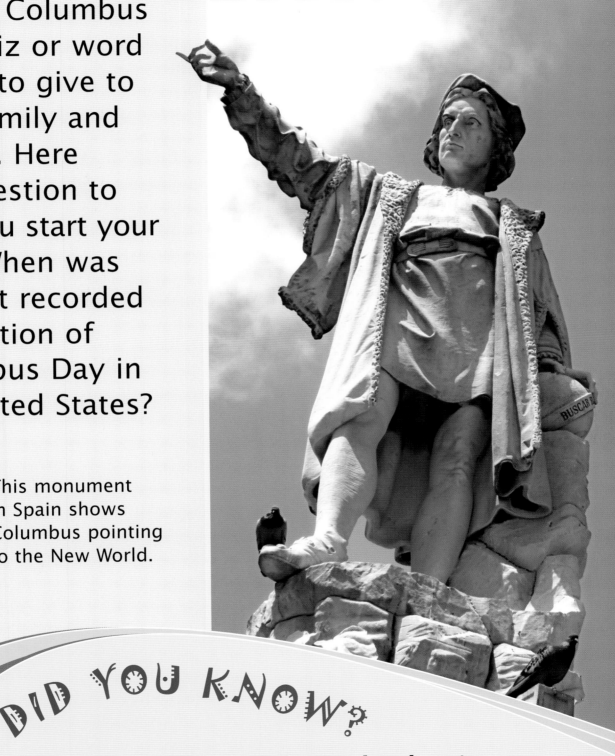

● This monument in Spain shows Columbus pointing to the New World.

DID YOU KNOW?

The monument of Christopher Columbus in Barcelona, Spain, is 196 feet (60 meters) high.

31

Glossary

colonization To establish a colony in or on an area of land

convert To change from one belief to another

federal A form of government

flagship The ship carrying the commander of a group of ships

heritage Something acquired from the past

indigenous Living naturally in a particular region or environment

merchant Someone who buys and sells goods

mistreated Treated badly

replicas Copies

settlement A newly settled place or region

slavery The state of being under the control of another person

uncivilized Lacking culture or refinement

voyages Journeys from one place to another, especially by water

Index

32